FINANCIAL ACCOUNTABILITY COACH

The Practical Guide To Goals Based Investing, Reaching Your Money Saving Goals And Hacks

MOSS JOLAS

DEDICATION

To the Glory of God.

CONTENTS

ACKNOWLEDGMENTS

Special thanks to all those who contributed to the successful completion of this financial research work.

INTRODUCTION

In the fast-paced world of money, financial stability and prosperity can be difficult to achieve. A trustworthy and effective guidance is needed as people work to safeguard their financial future. Welcome to "Financial Accountability Coach," your complete guide to goals-based investment, money-saving, and financial tricks.

This well-constructed guide takes us on a transformative financial journey beyond typical counsel. This book is your personal coach, helping you take charge of your finances beyond budgeting and investment methods. These sections offer advice for everyone, whether you're starting off or optimizing your financial strategy.

Goals-Based Investing Revealed:

Understanding goals-based investment fundamentals is key to financial success. "Financial Accountability Coach" simplifies investing strategies and helps you achieve your goals. From short-term milestones to long-term objectives, learn how to invest for your financial goals.

Achieving Your Saving Goals:

Saving money involves strategy and discipline, not just frugality. This guide covers saving with actionable suggestions and specific approaches to help you develop and maintain a savings plan.

Financial Success Hacks:

Personal finance is constantly changing, so keeping ahead requires finding new tricks and tactics. "Financial Accountability Coach" offers innovative and tried-and-true methods to boost financial efficiency. This book will help you remain ahead in the financial game by using technology and unusual savings approaches.

Prepare for a financial empowerment transformation. The book "Financial Accountability Coach" is your financial success companion. Accept the principles within and start your financial independence path.

CHAPTER 1

BUILDING THE FOUNDATION FOR FINANCIAL ACCOUNTABILITY

1.1 KNOWING YOUR FINANCES

Income, expenditure, assets, and obligations may be unfamiliar area in personal finance. You must understand your money to be financially healthy. Understanding your finances, making sensible choices, and building excellent financial habits are required.

1. Income: Income is vital to your finances. Finding and maximizing revenue is crucial. This includes your primary income, side employment, investments, etc. Diversifying income stabilizes and boosts earnings.

2. Budgeting: Budgeting involves financial planning. It involves budgeting, saving, and planning discretionary expenditure. A well-planned budget helps allocate resources and avoid financial blunders.

3. Cost analysis is essential for financial awareness.

Splitting expenditures into fixed and variable helps you cut or optimize. Tracking spending aids lifestyle and financial decisions.

4. Establishing and maintaining an emergency fund offers financial stability. Life is unpredictable, therefore costs may arise. An emergency fund keeps you financially safe from unexpected events.

5. Manage debt: Understand your situation. This includes knowing your debts, interest rates, and repayment schedule. Focusing on high-interest payments and getting them off can boost your finances.

6. Investments: Financial sustainability requires exploring investment alternatives. Stocks, bonds, real estate, and other assets require risk and return analysis. Investment diversification decreases risk and boosts earnings.

7. Retirement Planning: Financial security depends on retirement planning. Understanding and contributing to 401(k), IRA, and pension plans ensures financial stability.

8. Insurance Coverage: Protect your finances. This includes health, life, property, and other insurances to decrease risks and prevent disasters.

9. Financial objectives: Prioritizing financial goals sets financial milestones. Setting home, school, or early retirement objectives helps you succeed financially.

10. Continuous Learning: Investment alternatives, tax limits, and economic movements keep changing in finance. Continuous personal finance learning keeps you current in the financial world.

1.2 SETTING CLEAR AND ACHIEVABLE MONEY SAVING GOALS

Saving for a trip, emergency fund, or debt payback can help you stay focused and motivated. This article helps you set realistic money-saving goals for financial success.

1. Assess Your Finances

You must understand your money before setting objectives. Check your income, expenditures, and debts for improvements. Know where your money goes to set reasonable goals. Track your spending and save using a budget.

3. Make Specific, Measurable, Time-bound Goals

Broad goals like "save money" rarely work. Set measurable, time-bound goals. Instead of just "save for a vacation," specify the amount, date, and monthly savings. This clarity helps measure development and commitment.

4. Prioritize Goals

Goals differ in urgency and importance. Sort goals by financial impact. A luxury vacation may be less important than an emergency fund. Setting priorities helps you prevent over distributing resources.

5. Break big ambitions into smaller milestones.

Overwhelming financial goals might demoralize. Divide major goals into smaller ones. Set quarterly $2,500 savings goals to save $10,000 for a house down payment. These small wins will boost your confidence and keep you on pace.

6. Consider probable problems

Expect challenges in saving money. Unexpected expenses, income fluctuations, and personal issues may impair your ambitions. Have a backup for these issues. Be resilient and committed to your financial objectives by preparing for setbacks.

7. Create a realistic timeframe

Setting objectives and deadlines is important, but so is being realistic about their duration. Rushing to meet unrealistic deadlines might lead to financial blunders and exhaustion. Consider income, expenditures, and other obligations while defining a timeline. Adjust your objectives to be tough yet doable.

8. Track progress regularly.

To stay on track and make changes, track progress. Check your finances monthly, compare your savings to your goals, and assess any changes. Celebrate wins, identify development areas, and change goals using this data.

9. Change lifestyle and expenditure.

Money-saving goals often require lifestyle and spending changes. Reduce needless spending by dining out less, canceling subscriptions, or buying generics. Focus savings on finances. These improvements require discipline, but the long-term benefits are worth it.

10. Seek Professional Advice

Expert advice can help you achieve your goals and manage complex finances. Financial advisors provide customized guidance. They can help you define goals, strategize, and evaluate investment and debt management solutions.

1.3 THE ROLE OF ACCOUNTABILITY IN FINANCIAL SUCCESS

People of diverse backgrounds and ambitions covet wealth. From wealth accumulation to financial freedom to a happy retirement, financial success requires multiple strategies. Accounting is key to financial success.

Understanding Accountability: Financial success entails taking responsibility for actions and outcomes. Budgeting, saving, investing, and debt management are required. Responsible people make informed financial decisions that support their goals.

Setting realistic objectives is the first step to financial accountability. Set SMART goals to save for a house down payment, a child's education, or a comfortable retirement. As benchmarks, these goals guide financial decisions.

Financial accountability requires budgeting. Making a budget involves outlining income, expenditure, and savings goals. Tracking spending and sticking to a budget helps people understand finances.

Transparency helps them prioritize, manage, and alter resources, improving financial performance.

Established and maintained emergency funds are accountable for financial resilience. Medical emergencies, vehicle repairs, and job loss are covered by emergency funds. Emergency fund contributions and maintenance accountability enhances financial resilience, preventing unforeseen occurrences from interrupting plans.

Responsible debt management requires accountability. Personal accountability is needed for educational loans, credit card debt, and mortgages. Accountability requires regular payments, debt avoidance, and debt repayment plans. Financial responsibility improves credit and finances.

Successful investment requires accountability for decisions to build wealth. Discover financial options, risk tolerance, and realistic expectations. Maintaining investment portfolios in response to changing situations displays financial ambition.

Constant Learning and Flexibility: Economic conditions, tax restrictions, and investment opportunities change constantly in finance. Accountability for financial success requires ongoing modification. Monitoring financial trends, receiving professional help, and changing strategy are needed to achieve and sustain financial goals.

A Call For Short Review On Amazon

Thank you very much for reading this book. Enjoying this book so far or receiving value from it in anyway? Then, I would like to ask you for a favor to enable me reach more readers like you: kindly post a quick review for this book on its Amazon page.

When you get to the book page on Amazon, gently scroll down the page till you reach "Write A Customer Review" and click on it.

Thank you and God bless.

FINANCIAL ACCOUNTABILITY COACH

CHAPTER 2

EFFECTIVE GOAL-BASED INVESTING

2.1 INVESTMENT FUNDAMENTALS

People make money via investing. Even though money is scary, understanding investing fundamentals is crucial for financial stability. This lesson teaches investment essentials for effective financial market navigation.

1. Financial Goals: Set goals before investing. Having financial objectives for retirement, a home, or your kids' school will help. Your risk tolerance and time horizon determine the assets that fulfill your goals.

2. Risk and Return: Understanding risk and return is crucial to investing. Higher rewards generally equal higher risk. Finance and risk must be balanced by investors. Investing conservatively may provide lesser profits, whereas risk-taking may yield higher returns.

Asset classes contain investments with different risk and return profiles. Major assets include bonds, stocks, and cash. Corporate stock ownership may offer significant rewards but high volatility. Bonds provide interest, offering stability. Money market funds and cash equivalents are secure, liquid investments.

3. Diversification reduces risk by spreading assets across asset classes. Poor investment performance can be mitigated by stocks, bonds, and other assets.

4. Equity, bond, mutual fund, and ETF investments. All have benefits and downsides. Bonds pay interest, but stocks provide ownership and dividends. Mutual funds and ETFs invest investor money in various assets.

5. Long-term perspective: Successful investors understand its importance. Patient investing may generate big gains despite market volatility. Focusing on long-term goals and avoiding emotional reactions to market volatility might assist investors.

6. Research and Due Diligence: Fully research before investing. Know business finances, economic trends, and market conditions. Follow global trends that may effect your investments. Knowing lets you choose wisely.

7. Monitoring and Rebalancing: Investing is

ongoing. Update your portfolio periodically. Rebalancing preserves asset allocation by buying or selling. Your portfolio stays within your risk tolerance and financial goals.

2.2 PERSONAL AND INVESTMENT GOALS

Wealth and financial goals depend on investment. Investments must support personal aspirations to work. Strategic alignment ensures financial decisions complement life goals and generate rewards. This post will explain why investing with personal objectives is important and provide a plan to help people build purpose-driven investments.

Knowing Personal Goals:

Set personal goals before addressing investing alignment. These goals may include retirement preparation, generational wealth growth, property ownership, education, and dream vacations. Supporting socially responsible companies or the environment may be ethical.

After personal goals, strategic asset allocation follows. Depending on risk tolerance, time horizons, and financial goals, diversify investments across classes. Young professionals nearing retirement may invest more in growth assets like shares, while those closer to retirement may spend more in capital preservation.

Aligning investing with personal goals requires risk tolerance. A balance between financial and emotional goals is needed since risk tolerance differs. Effective risk management needs diversification, portfolio evaluations, and asset adjustments to match changing personal circumstances and aspirations.

Consider Time Horizon: Time horizon shapes investment strategy. Equity investments may expand and recover from market swings, which may support long-term goals. Short-term goals may require more liquid assets to lessen market volatility.

Tax preparation is needed to connect investments with personal goals. Investment tax effects can greatly impact outcomes. Tax-privileged accounts, investments, deductions, and credits can improve after-tax returns and assist attain financial goals.

As goals and finances change, portfolio reviews must be done frequently. This involves tracking investment performance, adjusting asset allocations, and aligning strategy with goals. Portfolio rebalancing at regular intervals restores risk profile and asset allocation.

Some investors attach assets to personal interests beyond finances. ESG and ethics affect decision-making. More meaningful investments are in companies that share one's values.

2.3 COMPREHENSIVE INVESTMENT STRATEGY

Long-term financial success involves careful investing. An ever-changing financial environment requires a well-planned approach that meets your financial goals, risk tolerance, and time horizon. This article helps you balance diversity, risk management, and long-term gain in your investing plan.

I. Set financial goals

First set financial goals before investing. Building wealth, retiring, buying a property, or paying for school? Goals will influence your financial plan. Every goal should have a timeline and cost to help you prioritize and manage resources.

Tolerate Risk:

Investing depends on risk tolerance. Consider age, income, investment skills, and emotional resilience. Knowing your risk tolerance helps pick portfolio investments. Younger, longer-term investors may be more daring, whereas older investors may be more conservative.

A solid investment plan requires diversification. Diversifying across asset classes, industries, and locales reduces portfolio damage from disastrous investments. Risk is reduced and rewards are more reliable.

Select Asset Allocation:

Financial success demands the right asset mix. The classic risk-return trade-off implies that higher rewards increase risk. Invest strategically depending on risk tolerance and financial goals. Portfolios with equities for growth and bonds for stability are balanced. Rebalance your portfolio when markets shift to maintain asset allocation.

V. Assess often:

Market conditions change frequently in finance. Check your investment strategy often to ensure it meets your goals and risk tolerance. Life changes, economic changes, and investing landscape changes may need adjustments. Follow market movements, economic statistics, and global events that may effect your holdings.

VI. Prioritize Long-Term Growth: Investing takes time and dedication. Avoid market-based snap judgments. Although market volatility is inevitable, well-diversified portfolios generally recover. Focus on long-term investment growth for compounding.

Be prepared for emergencies and liquidity before investing. An emergency reserve prevents premature investment liquidation. Portfolio liquidity allows you invest in market downturns.

CHAPTER 3

NAVIGATING THE MONEY-SAVING MAZE

3.1 BUDGETING BLISS: PRACTICAL BUDGET

Budgeting is essential for financial security. This method makes budgeting easy for financial success. Adapting your budget to your lifestyle and goals might help you handle unexpected surprises.

Know Your Money:

Any good budget starts with a comprehensive financial review. Salary, bonuses, and extras should be listed.

Setting Realistic Goals:

Budgeting without a goal is like floating aimlessly. Plan your budget with short- and long-term goals. Set objectives like a dream vacation, emergency money, or debt payback. Set ambitious but achievable objectives given your finances and future plans.

Categorizing and Funding:

Organize expenditures by cost. This streamlines

planning and money outflow control. Common expenses include housing, transit, groceries, entertainment, and debt. Balance essential and discretionary expenditures by allocating revenue to each category.

Consider the 50/30/20 Rule for balanced budgeting. Housing, electricity, and groceries use 50% of your budget. Leisure and eating account for 30% of spending. With 20% remaining, save and pay debt. This practical rule helps you budget for health and happiness.

Tracking and Adjusting:

Effective budgeting requires adaptability. Compare your spending against the budget to find patterns and improvements. Budgeting tools and spreadsheets make this easier and show real-time money. To maintain financial harmony, adjust allocations if a category routinely overspends.

This net prevents financial shocks. Keep a portion of your budget for long-term savings and investments to secure your financial future and make money work for you.

3.2 SMART SAVING TIPS FOR ALL INCOMES

Success and financial stability require saving. Smart saving may preserve your financial future regardless of income. This post will explore effective saving techniques for different income levels so anybody may be financially secure.

Low-income people:

1. Budget: o Track revenue and spending using a detailed budget.

Prioritize necessities and budget discretionary spending.

2. Emergency Fund: Save a small amount regularly.

High-interest savings accounts pay more.

Look into government subsidies to boost income.

Use community resources and support networks.

Find ways to reduce or eliminate non-essential spending to lower costs.

Shop smart, buy generics, and look for deals.

Mid-Income People:

1. Automate savings: Set up automatic transfers to a separate account.

Use employer-sponsored retirement and matching plans.

2. Debt Repayment: Limit interest payments by paying off high-interest debt first.

Consider debt consolidation for easier payments.

3. Investing: Diversify to lower risk.

Consider low-cost index funds for long-term growth.

4. Use employee benefits: HSAs and FSAs.

Optimize tax-favored 401(k)s and IRAs.

Rich People:

1. Tax Planning: Reduce taxes by planning income.

Consult a tax expert for tax-saving tips.

2. Advanced Investing: Consider real estate, private equity, and venture capital options. Consult a financial advisor for personalized strategies.

3. Charitable Giving: Benefit from gift tax deductions.

Create a strategic philanthropy donor-advised fund.

4. Estate Planning: Plan thoroughly to protect assets and decrease taxes.

Review and update beneficiaries regularly.

Strategies for All Incomes:

1. Financial Education: Learn about personal finance and investment.

Get financial guidance from seminars or professionals.

2. Try side businesses for extra cash.

Consider working extra to make money.

3. Review and adjust: Monitor your financial goals and adjust your savings plan.

Cost-reassess and find improvements.

4. Shop smart and negotiate bills, interest rates, and fees to save money.

Use discounts, loyalty programs, and rewards to

shop intelligently.

3.3 OVERCOMING COMMON SAVING CHALLENGES

Saving money is crucial to financial security, yet many individuals struggle to save. You may enhance your finances by confronting these problems.

Saving might be tough due to low income and high prices. Check your monthly spending to remedy this. Reduce or replace without lowering quality of life. Negotiate a raise, freelance, or work part-time to increase income. Budget savings may result from optimizing both sides.

2. Impulse spending and budgeting impair savings. Make a detailed budget with fixed and variable spending to avoid this. Set and follow a discretionary spending budget. Test non-essential purchases against your financial goals a day before buying. A well-planned budget helps you save and make smart choices.

3. Debt Repayment Issues:

High-interest debt can make saving difficult, especially if it consumes a lot of income. Be strategic about debt repayment. Consolidate high-interest bills, negotiate lower rates, or employ debt reduction programs. Make a realistic debt payback strategy and set aside money for it. Save more to obtain financial stability faster while you pay off debt.

4. Insufficient Emergency Fund: Unexpected expenditures may impede savings efforts. Start with an emergency fund to interrupt the cycle. Start $500 and build to cover three to six months' living expenses. Non-negotiable budget item: monthly emergency fund contribution. A financial cushion protects you from unforeseen events and encourages savings.

5. Investing Fear: This common barrier slows wealth growth. Know your investing options, risk tolerance, and financial goals. Get financial guidance from a pro. Grow your portfolio from low-risk, diverse assets as you grow comfortable. Capital accumulation and financial ambitions beyond savings involve overcoming investing fear.

CHAPTER 4

HACKS AND STRATEGIES FOR FINANCIAL SUCCESS

4.1 INCOME INCREASE

Maximum income in today's competitive market is key to financial success and security. Strategy may boost income and financial well-being, whether you're starting off or advancing. This article offers techniques to increase revenue and succeed financially.

1. Invest in Education and Skills: Learning enhances economic potential. Education and skill development boost industrial relevance and marketability. Higher degrees, certifications, and workshops and seminars provide in-demand skills.

2. Negotiate pay: Negotiate your salary to maximize income. Research industry standards and demonstrate your value to the firm. Negotiating job offers and performance reviews may increase your compensation.

3. Diversify revenue streams: Relying on one revenue source may slow financial growth. Starting a side business, investing in stocks or real estate, or freelancing helps diversify your income. Diversification safeguards and improves

profitability.

4. Build a Strong Professional Network: Networking is essential for career advancement. Build professional relationships through business networking, internet organizations, and peer interaction. Strong networks may provide opportunities, collaborations, and jobs.

5. Professional Strategy: Maximize earnings with wise professional choices. Consider higher-paying employment, leadership, or industry changes. Regularly assess your career and consider calculated income increases.

6. Financial Planning and Budgeting: Income optimization involves planning and budgeting. Set financial objectives and manage resources in a budget. Secure your financial future and benefit from long-term growth by saving and investing.

7. Increase productivity and streamline labor via technology and automation. Automation may help you manage work, take on more, and earn more. Stay updated on industry tech to stay ahead.

8. Continuous Performance Improvement: Achieve

greatness by improving. Exceeding expectations may lead to promotions, increases, and business recognition. Develop a growth mindset and seek feedback to improve.

9. Negotiate perks and benefits: Negotiate benefits and incentives with compensation. Health insurance, retirement plans, flexible work, and other advantages increase pay. Consider non-monetary benefits when computing earnings.

4.2 TECH-SMARTER MONEY MANAGEMENT

Personal finance changes constantly and technology has transformed money management. Fintech tools like budgeting apps and robo-advisors help customers make smart financial decisions and take charge. Technology has changed money management, and this essay discusses key tools and trends that are guiding financial success.

1. Personal Finance Apps: Digital Budgeting Revolution

Paper spending tracking is dead. Personal financial apps are vital for money management. Mint, YNAB, and PocketGuard categorize transactions and provide real-time financial insights. These apps provide personalized budgeting advice and show spending trends to assist users make money decisions.

2. AI/Predictive Analytics

Money management has improved using AI and predictive analytics. Data-driven AI financial tools identify patterns and provide actionable insights.

These technologies can predict expenditure, investment trends, and financial decision periods. Based on users' risk tolerance and financial goals, Wealthfront and Betterment use AI algorithms to build and manage diverse investment portfolios.

3. Contactless payments, digital wallets

Touchless payments and digital wallets have propelled cashless society. NFC and QR codes simplify transactions, making it easier to track spending and manage accounts in real time.

4. Blockchain, Cryptocurrencies

Blockchain and cryptocurrencies have transformed money management. Despite volatility, Bitcoin and Ethereum provide alternatives. Blockchain makes bitcoin transactions secure and transparent. Decentralised blockchains reduce costs and speed up financial transactions.

5. Smart Financial Education Platforms

Technological advancements have made financial education more accessible. Khan Academy and Investopedia educate budgeting and investing using interactive tools, videos, and quizzes. Financial knowledge and money judgments are improved by these platforms.

6. Active financial monitoring and warnings

Fast finance requires real-time data. Many banks and financial apps notify customers of questionable activity, low balances, and upcoming commitments in real time. This proactive approach helps people address potential issues promptly, eliminating financial setbacks and boosting money management.

7. Personal Financial Advice Chatbot

AI-powered chatbots provide personalized financial advice. These bots answer queries, educate budgeting, and recommend investments. Their 24/7 availability provides financial assistance whenever required. This customized approach boosts financial literacy and user experience.

4.3 UNEXPECTED FINANCIAL TIPS

A society concerned about financial stability is continuously seeking for innovative ways to produce money and secure a bright future. Traditional financial advice emphasizes planning, saving, and investing, but numerous unconventional yet effective financial hacks can boost your money. Ten unique strategies to make money and succeed are covered in this essay.

Minimalist lifestyle may be a financial trick, opposed to consumerist culture. Avoiding unnecessary expenses and focusing on the basics saves money and clarifies priorities. Sell or donate unneeded items to save or invest.

2. Cash-Only Life: Cash may change life in a digital era. Save for monthly and discretionary spending. This realistic strategy helps you budget and avoid debt by increasing expenditure awareness.

3. Gamify Savings: Make saving entertaining. Challenge yourself to fulfill financial goals on schedule. The positive reinforcement loop of milestone rewards makes saving exciting.

4. Negotiate everything: Many overlook the significance of daily negotiations. Negotiate rent, credit card interest, subscriptions, and medical bills. To retain customers, service providers compromise. Negotiating can save hundreds or thousands annually.

5. Start a second business to diversify your income. This might be freelancing, consultancy, or hobby income. Extra cash might be utilized for debt repayment, savings, or financial objectives.

6. Use cash-back credit cards responsibly. Buy cards that fit your lifestyle and provide the greatest cash back. Use these cards for everyday purchases and pay off the debt monthly to avoid interest and gain cash back.

7. House Hacking: Find inventive housing cost reductions. House hacking reduces living costs and offers passive income.

8. Barter and Skill Exchanges: Instead of buying, try trading products and services with community members. Trade skills or services for necessities. Conserving money and fostering cooperation.

9. Use tax-efficient investment to increase earnings.

10. Prioritize Experiences: While saving for the future is commonly advised, investing in meaningful experiences can enhance well-being. Spend money on fun to be balanced.

CHAPTER 5

THE ACCOUNTABILITY COACH APPROACH

5.1 COACH FOR FINANCIAL ACCOUNTABILITY

Financial travels are like new seas. The path to wealth, debt repayment, or financial goals is arduous and full with obstacles. Accountability coaches may change the game in tough conditions. Accountability coaches encourage and hold people accountable for their finances. Accountability coaches shape and improve financial paths in complicated ways.

Accountability coaches help customers set realistic financial goals. Goals guide financial decisions.

2. Developing a Practical Financial Plan: Accountability coaches assist clients create a realistic financial plan after setting goals. This strategy covers income, debt, expenditure, and savings. A detailed financial analysis helps the coach manage resources, regulate expenditure, and save toward goals.

3. Effective Budgeting: Financial management requires budgeting. Accountability coaches establish and execute budgets. This involves saving money,

allocating funds, and planning sustainable expenditure. Coaches aid with budgeting evaluations and changes.

4. Overcoming Financial Obstacles: Financial journeys may be difficult. Accountability coaches help with financial losses. After a job loss, medical emergency or unexpected expense, the coach helps identify solutions, adjust the financial plan, and stay focused on long-term goals.

5. Behavioral Coaching and Mindset Shifts: Accountability coaches go beyond numbers and spreadsheets to address money management behaviors. Money mindset and behavior must change for sustainability. The coach helps consumers identify and alter problematic financial habits, promoting proactive money management. The behavioral coaching stops overspending, impulsive financial judgments, and a healthy financial outlook.

6. Progress reviews: Regular reviews are key to financial success. An accountability coach monitors financial goals, budgets, and highlights accomplishments. These assessments allow financial

plan tweaks to keep the trip on track and reflect changing living conditions.

7. Educating and Empowering Clients: Financial knowledge may lead to long-term prosperity. Customers learn financial ideas and methods from an accountability coach. Empowerment offers people the knowledge and skills to make informed financial decisions, giving them confidence.

5.2 ACCOUNTABILITY PARTNER SELECTION

The right accountability partner can help us achieve our goals. Accountability partners support and hold us to our promises. This dynamic contact improves personal and professional progress. This study will examine accountability relationships and how to find the best one for you.

Being aware of accountability's impact

1. Shared goals and values

Finding an accountability partner with similar goals and beliefs is vital. Teaming up on health, professional, or artistic objectives develops support. Common goals foster friendship and understanding.

2. Skills that complement each other

Accountability relationships flourish with shared goals and complementary skills. Consider a partner whose strengths complement your weaknesses and vice versa. This synergy balances problem-solving with goal-setting.

3. Communicating Well

Successful accountability collaboration requires open communication. Partners should feel comfortable communicating thoughts, problems, and progress. Regular meetings or informal chats strengthen relationships and keep everyone informed.

4. Dependability, consistency

Accountability partnership success requires dependability. Trust your spouse to keep promises and vice versa. Accountability fosters trust and professional growth.

5. Praise and advice

Responsible accountability partners provide constructive feedback and support. Positive reinforcement and constructive criticism foster growth in both parties.

Choose an Accountability Partner

Identify your needs and goals

Determine your goals and needs before seeking accountability. You can find a partner who shares your goals by knowing them.

2. Develop personal and professional networks

Find accountability partners in your personal and business networks. Acceptable people include friends, coworkers, mentors, and family. Consider folks who share your goals and provide new perspectives.

3. Assess Compatibility

Compatibility goes beyond shared values. Communication, work, and time restrictions matter. A good relationship has similarities and differences to assist collaborate.

4. Set limits and expectations

Set explicit limits and expectations. Share check-ins, communication styles, and partner involvement. Set these guidelines to avoid misunderstandings and build a good relationship.

5. Trial Period Assess relationship fit and effectiveness. This helps both parties evaluate and improve. If trial collaboration succeeds, you may proceed confidently.

5.3 REGULARLY CHECK ACCOUNTABILITY:

Coaches provide structure and support for personal and professional goals. Accountability coaches guide and check in often. This inquiry will analyze the benefits of the accountability coach technique and how to construct a growth-promoting routine.

Accountability Coach Method

First, define the accountability coach role

Accountability coaches advise, inspire, and plan to keep individuals on track. Accountability coaches stress regular check-ins to build a feedback loop for lasting progress, unlike traditional mentorship.

2. Building trust and rapport

Accountability coaching requires coach-client trust and rapport. Successful coaching partnerships require open communication and respect. Sharing successes, challenges, and chances for growth requires trust.

3. Goal-setting and clarity

Clear goals drive accountability coaching. Coaching

helps clients set SMART goals. This goal-setting process leads coaching and matches client and coach expectations.

4. Create a supportive environment

A supportive accountability coach helps individuals take responsibility. This positive environment helps people to overcome obstacles, learn from mistakes, and succeed. As cheerleader, the coach fosters resilience and determination.

Establishing Regular Check-Ins

1. Regularity and

Coaching accountability requires regular check-ins. A check-in mechanism is needed to maintain momentum. For coach and client convenience, choose daily, weekly, or bi-weekly. Regular check-ins enable real-time progress tracking and changes.

2. Agenda Structure

Each check-in should be scheduled for efficiency and effectiveness. Assess progress, acknowledge triumphs, and resolve problems since the last check-in. Discuss, prioritize, and develop goals at this time. A plan directs the coaching session.

3. Communication Open

Open up check-ins. The coach and client should feel comfortable discussing concerns and insights. Create a nonjudgmental forum for advice, opinions, and experiences. Effective communication enhances coaching and teamwork.

4. Reassessing and tweaking goals

Goals can be adjusted at regular checkpoints. Changes in circumstances may change ambitions. Accountability coaches regularly evaluate relevant and achievable goals. Coaches can customize courses for customers.

5. Honorable Progress and Results

Celebrate successes during check-in. Recognition of little wins promotes healthy behavior and goal-setting. This celebration makes coaching more fun for coach and client.

CHAPTER 6

OVERCOMING CHALLENGES AND STAYING ON TRACK

6.1 FINANCIAL MISTAKES TO AVOID

Personal finance management is essential to pleasure and security. However, various challenges might derail financial achievement. We will examine common financial errors and how to prevent them to build a sound financial foundation.

1. Insufficient Emergency Fund

Insufficient emergency funds are a common financial blunder. Unexpected medical or auto repair bills might come anytime. Without a cash cushion, unforeseen expenses may need high-interest loans.

Overcoming Strategy: Emergency fund three to six months' living expenses. Put this money first to avoid financial problems.

2. Beyond Means

Spending more than earning causes financial problems. This usually leads to debt, which can quickly grow and hurt long-term finances.

Overcoming Strategy: Realistic budgets help you understand income, expenses, and discretionary spending. Tracking expenditures, prioritizing needs over wants, and making sensible financial decisions may stop living beyond means.

3. Ignoring Retirement Planning

Many delay retirement preparation, assuming they have time.

Overcoming Strategy: Start retirement savings early. Time and compound interest may improve retirement savings.

4. Interest-laden debt

Overcoming Strategy: Pay off high-interest debt fast. Create a debt repayment strategy and get professional aid to speed things up.

5. Finance Literacy Gap

Financial literacy is low, preventing people from making informed financial decisions. Without budgeting, investment, and credit management expertise, people may make unwise financial decisions.

Overcoming: Study finance. Study, take seminars, and consult financial specialists. Financial knowledge helps people make sensible long-term decisions.

6. Ignoring insurance needs

Ineffective insurance management is another financial trap. Illness, accidents, and property damage can cost a lot without insurance.

Overcoming Strategy: Get health, life, property, and income insurance. Update policies to suit current conditions.

6.2 LIFE CHANGE PLAN ADJUSTMENT

Life's surprises might affect your money. You must adapt your financial approach to life circumstances to achieve financial stability and long-term goals. This conversation will cover modifying your financial strategy to life changes and resiliency.

1. Life Fluidity

Life throws milestones, hardships, and surprises. To achieve your financial goals, you must modify your financial plan to employment changes, family growth, health concerns, and financial losses.

2. Common Life Changes: Financial

Proactive financial planning starts with understanding common life events that may influence your finances. Changes include:

A. Career Transitions: Promotions, job changes, and career transfers influence income, benefits, and retirement.

a. Family Changes: Budgeting, insurance, and long-term planning must alter for marriage, divorce, childbirth, and family structure.

c. Health Problems: Unexpected health issues might cause medical costs, employment changes, and insurance demands.

Moving, buying, or downsizing might influence mortgage payments, property taxes, and housing prices.

3. Regular Financial Checkup Value

Regular financial checks let you evaluate your plan and find improvements. Review your financial goals, budget, and investment strategy annually or after important life events with these inspections.

4. Adjusting Financial Plan

a. Reevaluate financial goals: Life changes may involve reevaluating short- and long-term financial goals. Update goals when priorities change.

b. Review and Adjust Your Budget: Income, spending, and family structure might affect it. Assess your spending, cut unnecessary spending, and reallocate funds to achieve your new financial goals.

Review Insurance Coverage: Life changes need

insurance evaluations. Check your health, life, property, and other insurance plans for coverage.

Update Your Emergency Fund: Life changes might generate financial concerns. Your emergency fund should cover unexpected bills and match your daily expenses.

f. Income and employment changes may require retirement contribution modifications. Take advantage of employer-sponsored programs and invest in retirement to ensure your future.

Realign Investments: Your risk tolerance, financial goals, and time horizon may need portfolio realignment. Talk to a financial advisor to make sure your investments fit your new goals.

Life changes might affect debt management. Reduce financial stress by prioritizing high-interest payments and planning payback.

5. Get help from professionals

Major life transitions may benefit from professional financial counsel. Financial advisers provide tailored solutions, insights, and help with difficult financial decisions. Financial advisers can help you make informed, goal-oriented work, buying, and family decisions.

6. Gain financial flexibility

A flexible financial basis demands resilience. This requires an emergency reserve, diversification, and flexibility. An adaptable financial plan can handle life's shocks.

7. Monitor and adjust regularly

Financial strategy changes require ongoing monitoring and adjustment. Regularly review your finances, budget, and investments. Financial flexibility helps you stay on track when life changes.

6.3 MOTIVATION

Financial success has highs and lows, and setbacks are inevitable. Financial setbacks like job loss, unexpected costs, and economic downturns can depress. Staying motivated and resilient throughout bad times is key to long-term success. This research will evaluate frequent financial failures and give motivation and guidance.

Financial Setback Awareness

1. Job loss and income drop

Lost income or employment is a financial calamity. It can influence savings, financial stability, and future uncertainty. People must adapt quickly and make wise financial decisions to withstand job loss or income drop.

2. Unexpected costs and crises

Medical emergencies, vehicle repairs, and housing maintenance may derail even the finest budgets. People without emergency reserves may suffer with unforeseen bills.

3. Stock market volatility, investment losses

Investors often struggle with market volatility and losses. Economic and market downturns can depress portfolio values, hurting long-term financial goals. Market fluctuations must be withstood to stay motivated.

4. Credit card, loan, and mortgage debt can be a huge impediment.

Ways to Stay Inspired

1. Review and Adjust Goals

Reassessing and revising short- and long-term financial goals is essential following financial setbacks. Adjust goals to current conditions instead of discarding them. Setting achievable goals may inspire and regulate finances.

2. Budget realistically

Financial setbacks can need reassessing spending and budgeting. A realistic budget that fits existing finances can help you overcome problems. Save, cut non-essentials, and prioritize pressing concerns.

3. Save more emergency funds

Money problems emphasize the need for an

emergency fund. Don't have an emergency fund? Start one for three to six months' living expenses. This financial cushion may ease your mind and safeguard you in hard times.

4. Get help from professionals

Financial consultants assist with financial issues. Financial advisers tailor budgeting, debt management, and investing. People may make decisions and overcome challenges with their counsel.

5. Prioritize controls

Focusing on internal losses may empower, even if financial losses are uncontrollable. This may require cutting spending, finding new money streams, or enhancing financial knowledge to make good choices.

6. Value mental and emotional wellbeing.

Financial stress can harm mental health. Focus on self-care and happiness. Fun and calming activities reduce stress and boost finances.

7. Diversify income

Diversify income sources following job loss or income reduction. This might be freelance, part-time, or entrepreneurial work. Income diversification might assist in harsh times.

8. Reevaluate Investment Strategies

Review and adapt investment plan for market volatility losses. Assess risk tolerance, asset allocation, and long-term investment portfolio alignment with a financial advisor.

A Call For Short Review On Amazon

Thank you very much for reading this book. Enjoying this book so far or receiving value from it in anyway? Then, I would like to ask you for a favor to enable me reach more readers like you: kindly post a quick review for this book on its Amazon page.

When you get to the book page on Amazon, gently scroll down the page till you reach "Write A Customer Review" and click on it.

Thank you and God bless.

CHAPTER 7

SUSTAINING FINANCIAL ACCOUNTABILITY FOR LONG-TERM SUCCESS

7.1 CELEBRATING SUCCESS

Financial success depends on acknowledging milestones and triumphs. Financial accountability involves reviewing progress, celebrating successes, and keeping motivated. Celebrating financial accountability may lead to long-term success.

Celebrating milestones matters

1. Drive and Momentum

Celebrate successes to keep motivated and financially on track. Celebrating financial milestones like paying off a significant debt, saving a goal, or accomplishing an investing objective keeps you making smart decisions.

2. Reward

Recognizing triumphs strengthens good financial habits. Results motivate people to meet financial goals. Financial control and empowerment arise from this reinforcement of behaviors and results.

3. Higher Wellbeing

Success in money boosts numbers and well-being. Celebrating anniversaries shows how much financial decisions have benefited life. Financial, emotional, and mental well-being may improve.

4. Building a Successful Culture

Celebrations in financial accountability boost success. For support and encouragement, celebrate family, partnership, or team achievements. Successful feelings promote collaboration and financial goal dedication.

5. Long-term outlook

Celebrate long-term financial planning accomplishments. It tells them that financial success takes time and several accomplishments. This method encourages patience and tenacity, crucial for financial success.

Achievement Recognition for Financial Accountability

1. Regular Reflection

Monitoring financial development helps identify accomplishments. Check financial goals and progress often. Recognition and appreciation of milestones emphasize work and success.

2) Set Goals

Financial responsibility needs measurable goals. Goals may include debt repayment, savings, or investment. Clear objectives help identify accomplishments and guide progress.

3. Celebrate small wins

Celebrating small wins is just as important. Every financial success, big or small, merits credit. Small victories like budgeting, paying off debt, or saving aid the trip.

4. Share achievements.

Sharing financial successes socializes recognition. Sharing triumphs with loved ones fosters responsibility and joy. Social support can boost success.

5. Create Traditions

Traditions around financial milestones give acknowledgment significance. Possibly a special lunch, weekend getaway, or family gathering. These customs celebrate financial achievement with enthusiasm, making the event more memorable and encouraging long-term success.

6. Record progress

People can track their financial performance in a journal, spreadsheet, or app. This document records financial goals and achievements. Reviewing this record may inspire you throughout trying times.

7. Set New Goals

After victories, set new targets to continue. Financial success requires setting, pursuing, and achieving goals. New goals create new challenges and growth opportunities, keeping the route exciting.

A case study: Celebrating milestones' impact

1. Debt Repayment Success Story

Imagine a person paying off many of credit cards. Celebrating this victory relaxes and inspires healthy financial habits. Success in one personal financial area can help others.

2. Emergency Fund Savings Milestone

Imagine a family that saves three months' living

expenses in an emergency fund. Recognition of this success enhances their financial security and confidence in overcoming unexpected challenges. This positive experience encourages people to save and develop their emergency funds for peace of mind.

7.2 CHANGING GOALS AND FINANCIAL PLANS

Financial planning evolves with life. As individuals age, goals and money change. You must detect and manage these changes to ensure your financial plan fulfills your current goals and provides a solid foundation for the future.

I. Understanding Goal Evolution (250 words): Life milestones include career, family, and retirement. Each level brings financial goal-related issues and opportunities. Updating your financial plan requires understanding how these goals evolve.

Early career objectives may include debt reduction, emergency fund building, and short-term savings. Family-building may shift priorities to house funds, kid education, and life insurance.

Financial strategies, healthcare, and income sustainability may be focused as retirement approaches. Understanding these shifts lets people adjust their financial strategy to meet current needs and plan for future milestones.

II. Regular Financial Health Assessments (300

words): Financial checkups help identify difficulties. Income, consumption, savings, assets, and debts are assessed. Analysis of your budget and spending patterns helps allocate resources and identify improvement opportunities.

Your investment strategy meets your long-term goals by monitoring portfolios and adjusting asset allocations based on risk tolerance and market conditions. Regular checks let you see how successfully your emergency fund and insurance cover financial risks.

III. Economic Change Adjustment (250 words): As the economy changes, inflation, interest rates, and market volatility may impact your finances. You must watch economic trends and adjust your financial plan.

Investing before inflation is crucial. Adapting debt management to interest rate changes may also help your finances. Flexibility with economic changes helps your financial plan weather setbacks.

Conclusion (100 words): You must constantly adjust your financial approach as goals change.

Being proactive, reassessing your financial health, and responding to economic changes may keep your financial plan robust and aligned with your life objectives. The iterative financial planning strategy delivers lifelong confidence and financial stability.

7.3 FINANCIAL WISDOM: LEGACY ACCOUNTABILITY

Financial advice passed down may bring generations of accountability and prosperity. Financial education is crucial in a world of economic unpredictability and shifting markets. This article explains how financial awareness may inspire responsibility and success.

The Basis of Financial Wisdom:

1. Money value is the foundation of financial knowledge: Teaching hard work, earning, and saving encourages financial responsibility. Teaching kids and heirs how each dollar is made instills accountability.

2. Budgeting and Financial Planning: These principles assist people manage resources. Showing the value of living within one's means and setting realistic financial goals promotes long-term stability versus short-term gain.

Legacy of Accountability:

Open family discussions about money are crucial to

passing on financial wisdom. By making budgeting, investment, and financial goals discussions safe, families may benefit from one other's challenges.

3. Lead by example: Actions speak louder than words. Teaching financial literacy by example works. To inspire future generations, save, invest, and avoid debt.

Third, financial repercussions must be taught to promote accountability. Discussing good and negative financial results helps people realize how their activities influence them.

4. Promoting Financial Education: Financial education empowers families for the future. Teach personal finance, investing, and economic trends. This knowledge aids financial decisions and responses.

Managing Challenges and Change:

Financial savvy includes preparation for economic uncertainty. Teaching resilience, adaptation, and emergency reserves helps people overcome obstacles without compromising finances.

Technology changes money management in the financial sector. Teaching technological adaption ensures future generations can use new tools and platforms to better their finances.

Conclusively, we finish our examination of financial responsibility coaching by emphasizing its impact on financial knowledge. After learning goals-based investing and several savings techniques, accountability is crucial to financial success.

Our practical guide guides you through personal finance's storms. It taught investing, savings, and financial planning. Financial accountability impacts families, communities, and generations beyond wealth growth.

One of our greatest legacies is wisdom. Remember that your financial decisions now affect your future as you follow this instruction. Accountability gifts loved ones, illuminate others, and prove financial wisdom's strength.

Goal-based investing anchors you in the fast-paced world of finance, where trends, markets, and economies shift. The unavoidable difficulties will be overcome by your unwavering financial goals and rigorous methods.

Remember that financial success is a marathon as you explore these recommendations. We require persistence, adaptation, and lifelong learning. Saving and investing builds a financial future that can weather the storms and last.

Consider how your financial decisions will affect your family and instill accountability. Share your achievements, failures, and lessons. Encourage the next generation to utilize money to attain goals and create opportunities.

A financial accountability coach is a lifestyle, not just a person. It's about financial management, wise choices, and inspiring others. Travel this route and recognize your change and its influence on others.

Finally, may your wealth inspire, endure, and instruct. Goal-based investing, money-saving goals, and practical techniques had lasting impact. A secure and successful future is brightened by financial responsibility.

A Call For Short Review On Amazon

Thank you very much for reading this book. Enjoying this book so far or receiving value from it in anyway? Then, I would like to ask you for a favor to enable me reach more readers like you: kindly post a quick review for this book on its Amazon page.

When you get to the book page on Amazon, gently scroll down the page till you reach ''Write A Customer Review'' and click on it.

Thank you and God bless.

You can reach me on reflects2015@gmail.com